❧ Morning and Evening Prayer in the Parish ❧

Laurence Mayer

LITURGY TRAINING PUBLICATIONS

Also available from

Liturgy Training Publications:

Evening Prayer: The Leader's Book

Participants' cards for Evening Prayer

Morning Prayer: The Leader's Book

Participants' cards for Morning Prayer

Copyright © 1985, Archdiocese of Chicago

Liturgy Training Publications
1800 North Hermitage Avenue
Chicago IL 60622-1101
312/486-7008

ISBN 0-930467-11-6

CONTENTS

FOREWORD

This small volume is a second step. The first was taken several years ago when LTP published *Evening Prayer in the Parish.* That text has been revised and enlarged and new material has been added. The approach has remained the same: a parish-based, simple ritual for the celebration of the turning points of the day.

Many congregations now celebrate vespers (often called evensong) on Sunday evenings during the seasons of Lent, Eastertime and Advent. Some have begun to do this year round. A few parishes have begun to see a service of morning prayer as the need and heritage of the local church, especially on weekdays. These introductory and explanatory notes will help parish liturgy planners and ministers as they seek to offer the church's ancient but lively heritage to parishioners.

The greater part of this text was written by Father Laurence Mayer. He was assisted in several chapters by Father Alan Scheible. Both are members of St. Norbert Abbey in De Pere, Wisconsin.

Evening Prayer: The Leader's Book and *Morning Prayer: The Leader's Book* are also available from LTP. They offer all the texts needed by presider and cantor for the celebration of the rites described here. In addition, prayer cards for the participants are available.

— Gabe Huck

1 ह

Response to the Day's Cycle

"Evening came and morning followed, the first day." The stillness of twilight and dawn signal by their special flavor that they are threshold moments. The world's hush at these times is not a poetic contrivance but a palpable reality before which creation hesitates and intently listens. Then it settles into rest or else steps off into activity. On these hinges the course of time swings from daylight into night, from dark into day.

Peoples of quite different ages and cultures acknowledge these moments as times of prayer. In the humble bow toward the rising or setting sun, in the Angelus of the laborer going to work and in the elaborate ceremonies of great temples and monasteries, in the rituals of all sorts, humans have shaped this pause, giving praise and thanks to God for the turning of the light. This variety of rites points to something of what evening and morning are about, transcending age, peoples, culture and place.

In the simple human feeling for these unique moments in the day's cycle, communities have found a basic rhythm and a form for their prayer. No authority can take credit for establishing the significance of morning and evening, much less their character as sacred times. Sunset and sunrise are sacred in and of themselves. Experiencing them, people know they have touched the forming and sustaining creator. In this touch, they also have come to

1

accept their common creatureliness with other beings. The sun's journey moves all living things like a vast tide, ebb and flow. Whether names like vespers and lauds are used or not, this remains true: people gather to pray, not because of a *law*, or in response to an *idea*, but in the *event/happening* of sunset and sunrise.

The roots of our traditional structures of morning and evening prayer are people intimate with "sun-time" and the changing seasons. For the Jewish people in biblical times, nature was filled with signs and voices announcing God's presence; in psalm after psalm, praise is sung with shaded moods of expression from fear to exuberant joy. The world shouted the grandeur of God. Light from the sun and light from fire spoke of the creating and supporting and protecting God. These expressed the sense of need, of dependence on an other. Early evidence for Christian daily prayer prescribes the recitation of the Lord's prayer three times a day—in the morning, at noon and again at night, making this prayer the equivalent of the S'hema: "Hear, O Israel, the Lord our God is one."

The *how* of the development of liturgies for morning and evening is lost to us. But we know that Christian rites did emerge once the conditions became favorable. A number of evening services are known by the fourth century from different places in the Near East. The impact of the monastic movement during and after this time did not erase the light-centeredness of this community prayer, although it was at times spiritualized. We see a shifting of attention from the ritual and nature symbols (the time of day, water, fire) to the recitation of and reflection upon texts from scripture, particularly the psalms. The liturgy of the hours (the "Divine Office") is permeated by this monastic spirituality. Even so, there are vestiges from other times, places, spirits, understandings. The liturgical hours contain the flotsam and jetsam of once-flourishing parochial traditions.

A lack of coherent structure in the official forms is one of the principal difficulties in reestablishing a parish daily prayer. In order to work well as a group activity, a basic structural integrity is needed in which the ritual is unified and flows from the occasion for the prayer. In the case of a daily prayer, the

2

occasion for prayer is simply the time of day. Text and action and material symbols must then have recognizable and appropriate links to one another. These are to be suggested from within rather than through an abstract ordering for the sake of some intended meaning.

Parish daily prayer can flourish among contemporary Christians and still be in continuity with the larger traditions of the church. The reason *these* people gather lies in their shared experience of an event, a mystery heralded in the time of day. The event itself suggests certain actions and responses, ritual expressions and symbols, some of which are so powerful and basic to the human condition that they transcend time and place in their relevance. Thus, bread and wine, water, light and darkness, fire, breath and the touch of human hands are not culturally determined. They are timeless, and their significance comes from our being human and creaturely. The "things" of prayer come from the experiences of life.

When looked at in this way, Christian daily prayer is found to be rooted in three related movements:

- praise to God for the presence of Christ, the source of life and light in the world

- the expression, in response to this gift, of the willingness to be converted from our lifelessness to God's life, from our darkness to God's light, from our chaos to a new creation

- as a body/church, we place the needs and concerns of the world before a compassionate God who renews all things in Christ

The divergence of this thematic outline for daily prayer from the traditional structure of the Divine Office is significant. In the latter form, the time of day is secondary rather than the essential cue for the prayer's form and meaning. A renewal of ritual elements suggested by the time of day (seen as the principal symbol for the events of salvation) is necessary for effective celebration.

The items incorporated here are drawn from ancient forms of vesper and lauds services. The argument for their use, however, does not rely on antiquity but on their appropriateness: they offer a way for us to respond to the day. A prayer service with only the basic elements would be quite brief. In the past, the liturgy was elaborated by using prayer texts, psalms, hymns, scripture canticles and readings, processions and ceremony. Yet, beneath the elaboration, the same interwoven themes mentioned above can be recognized and celebrated as creation's response to the saving presence of God — praise, conversion, intercession.

2 ॐ

Guidelines for Parish Morning and Evening Prayer

Although the *General Instruction on the Liturgy of the Hours* reasserts the need for a renewed parochial daily prayer, there are some rather enormous problems to be faced. If ignored or dismissed, they will insure the self-destruction of whatever attempts are made. These problems are more than the simple ones of scheduling and format; they are difficulties of catechesis, ecclesiology, social and liturgical dynamics. The urgency for reestablishing a lively daily prayer comes from the sacramental/experienced presence of God in creation. This is not a sense fostered by our culture, yet it is essential in the Catholic Christian way of life. In liturgy, the things of this world are the avenue through which the presence is experienced and touched. Bread, wine, fire, water, wood and stone, sunrise and sunset are symbols pregnant with life and spirit, awaiting the release of their vitality in the community's recognition and celebration. Time, no less than bread and wine, is the creature and gift of a generous, loving creator.

Perhaps the first hurdle, then, in establishing daily common prayer in the parish is this: to accept ourselves as "strangers in a strange land." Religious and clergy will need great caution so that they do not approach all of this as "old hat" (even if freshly cleaned and blocked). Fresh attention is necessary during the building process to avoid presuming patterns and practices which do not and cannot coincide with the content and dynamics of an authentic celebration. Below are some principles which might be helpful.

1. Daily Prayer is the celebration of evening and morning as events.

In any celebration, the community dynamics are fueled by an awareness of the occasion which supplies the motive for coming together. A community usually feels confident that it has the skills and knowledge and appropriate materials to do what it has set out to do, namely, to celebrate something particular. In the evening, we are cued by the day's passing to remember Jesus' own life moving through death and burial to resurrection. In the morning, the sun's rise and our reawakening is a creation/resurrection sign. Both evening and morning are memorial events. This memory is not of a past event but of a present time-and-space reality. Evening is a passover time when the Easter Triduum catches us up, pausing at the mystery of Holy Saturday and the resting in the tomb. It is our daily time of passover in the presence of Christ, the light who has gone ahead of us and who now stands as our light in the darkness. Similarly, morning is Easter, dawning with new life and the new creation warmed and illumined by Christ, the sun of justice.

Remember that it is the time of day, rather than the season or feast, that is primary to daily prayer. The particular shape that sunset and sunrise give to daily prayer should never be lost in trying to accommodate the season or feast.

2. Common prayer is the work of the whole community.

The ministers (ordained or otherwise) do not have the controlling interest. All of the arrangements, from the setting to the format, and all of the elements (lighting of candles, the hymn, incense offering, water blessing, gestures and movement, music) need eventually to be worked out with the group itself. That means *with* not *by*. The content and shape of a prayer service is not determined by consensus: *something already there* must be respected by the celebration and this implies certain stable elements in the form. The pastor or worship committee needs to

6

spend the time learning what these are. Planners will also be in a position to assess the resources and abilities available within the group, and to know what can be done now and what must wait for future addition or refinement.

Therefore, at the beginning, keep everything simple and direct, able to be understood without extended and repeated explanations. The watchword at the start is this: Less is more! Problems may signal the need for fewer words and cleaner actions/symbols.

The texts and basic pattern should be memorizable in the course of regular use. This implies a certain brevity and stability of elements, including the hymns. Hymns should be carefully selected for specific reference to the time of day and the content of the prayer, not chosen at random from a common pot of familiar items. Admittedly, the resources are slim at present, but suitable ones can be found. Learning a new hymn for each day is not wise when one or two of substance will bear long use. Remember the example which the popular devotions give: a hymn can become a real treasure and much loved, even when sung week after week for years. The content of the hymn is the important thing to watch. Changing the melody at different seasons will provide a relief from monotony, but don't leap too soon to the conclusion that "the people are tired of it." "People" seem to tire less easily than liturgy planners.

3. **Integrating each separate element of word and act with the intent of the whole is critical.**

The parts must stay in comfortable balance with each other. Give more attention to the essential expressions, but watch for overstatement. Trying to say too much quickly strains the celebration. More is not better, and flights of poetic fancy will blur or smother the intent of the celebration. Things which might move us in our personal and private prayer cannot be expected to move a group. Common prayer is not the place for individual ecstasy, especially when consciously engineered. Thus, excessively "churchy" hymns and music or gesture and vestments, or even psalms and readings which do not pertain to the time event may warm a sentimental piety, but at the same moment cripple the common celebration. Restraint and integrity are the words to heed.

4. Spontaneity is fine when it is well planned.

Off-the-top-of-head changes in patterns or prayers serve only to derail the internal flow of the rite and to upset unnecessarily the fine-tuning which individuals and community are trying to achieve. Particularly this is so when a new form is being learned: the group needs the discipline of close adherence to the structures until the fundamental patterns have had enough time to be internalized.

Once an effective ceremonial action is found, let it be for a while — a long while. If there has been care and attention to basics during the building time, the final shape will be eminently usable and suitable. The group will sense as a whole when it is time to do some adjusting.

5. The ritual actions are the core of the service.

Ritual actions are more powerful than words when they are carefully respected for themselves. If it should be necessary to abbreviate a rite, keep the action instead of the words. We tend to hold words in very high regard, but this does not always serve common prayer well. Symbols are opened to experience by actions, texts and setting. If a priority were to be laid out, the texts are secondary to the "stuff" of the symbol; i.e., that which grounds the symbol as an *experience* is prior to that which expresses its *meaning.* To abbreviate or eliminate the deed in favor of an elaborate text weakens the celebration. Beware also of the mentality that says: "Incense (or water or fire) means *this.* Period." The power of signs and symbols is in their ambiguity. Learning how to let them speak effectively requires patience from us.

6. Morning and evening prayer are celebrations in their own right.

Maintain the independence of morning and evening prayer from any other devotion or liturgy, e.g., benediction or holy hours before the blessed sacrament or eucharist. When possible, use a different space, one appropriate to the size of the group.

8

7. Whole persons celebrate common prayer.

We are moved to pray not by the abstractions in texts but by the here-and-now of our lives. One of the tasks of its prayer is to help the assembly uncover in their daily life the experiences of life, death, burial and resurrection already present and effective. These experiences flow through our individual and collective day, and in them we rediscover our mutual passover/passion in Jesus. Life, after all, is not an intellectual process. It is warm/cold, physical, tangible, emotional, spiritual, joyfilled and painful—altogether a *human* movement. Daily prayer recognizes this in its rich and steady use of symbol and in its involvement of the whole person through gesture, posture, song, word, silence.

3 ॐ

The Elements
of Evening Prayer

1. The Light Service or Lucernarium

In liturgy, the principal communication mode is the symbol; words are only one kind of symbol. For evening and morning prayer, the time of day is the primary symbol: sunset and sunrise. Time sensed through the circle of dusk, dark and dawn is nature's sign for the presence of its creator.

The *lucernarium* (from *lucerna*, lamp) grew from a Jewish home ritual of pre-Christian times: the lighting of the lamps on Sabbath eve. The Hebrew Scriptures abound in light images for the messiah, the light-to-come, the *oriens ex alto*. In the New Testament, Christ names himself "light of the world." Thus the light symbols of evening prayer—the sun and the candle—are more than coincidental to the celebration, and surely more than items in a nice atmosphere.

Evening prayer depends on these: the sunlight fading and the candle shining in the growing darkness. Thus, 1:30 PM is not an appropriate time for evening prayer, nor, for that matter, is late evening or bedtime. Let the chosen time be near sunset or when the light is noticeably declining so that the candle can establish its own place in the center of the assembly.

The celebration begins with the proclamation of the central event: "Jesus Christ is the light of the world!" Christ's advent expels the gathering darkness of these last days. A hymn in praise of that light intensifies and expands the proclamation. At its conclusion comes thanksgiving for the gift of Christ, our light. Even on great feasts and during the seasons of the church year, this clear focus on the light is to be preserved.

2. The Incense Service

As the burning candle stands in the half-light of early evening, a sign of the presence of Christ, our call to repentance and conversion is expressed by the incense offering. The psalm which accompanies this action, Psalm 141, once was a fixed element of the evening office. The refrain is: "Let my prayer, O Lord, rise like incense before you, the raising of my hands like an evening sacrifice." These words refer to the sacrifice offered morning and evening in the temple at Jerusalem in expiation for the sins of the people.

Burning and smoke are full of ambiguity. They show destruction but their other face reveals them to be cleansing and purifying. Evening elicits reflections on the course of our day's affairs. The sun's setting allows nature to raise questions about this day, our values, our own transience/pilgrimage. Our concerns *do* dissipate like smoke. And we trust that the evil and hurt which we have worked, wittingly or not, will not track us down in the dark. The smoking incense can say more than words about humanness and human events.

The burning of incense, not the psalm, is the essential sign. If it should be necessary to abbreviate the rite, keep the action rather than the words.

3. Intercessions

Whenever the church gathers for worship, we commend our care and concern for all of creation to the Father through the person of Christ. These prayers of the faithful are an expression of what it means to be baptized into Christ: we are a people set apart, but aware of our needs and limitations. Just as Christ continually stands on our behalf before his Father, so we intercede continually for the world. The reintroduction of these prayer-litanies into the Mass and other public worship services is, in part, intended to reestablish our identity as a community at

12

worship. In liturgy, this community is *ecclesia:* the *called from/gathered together* ones. Individuals have set aside their prerogatives as private persons to acknowledge that they are members of one body.

Intercessions are a universal, concrete and inclusive voicing of the real concerns of this body for all that is. In them, we accept responsibility and accountability for the return of everything to the loving and creating God from whom all things come. Reference to a special feast or anniversary may be made within the intercessions, but this requires careful preparation.

The Lord's prayer is the church's own prayer and deserves to be spoken or sung whenever we assemble. In the form of service presented here, it customarily precedes the blessing.

The assembly is then dismissed in peace.

4 ❧

The Celebration of Evening Prayer

Evensong, as the evening prayer is sometimes called, is a prayer of thanksgiving, repentance and petition. We praise the redeeming presence of Christ, the light, and ask his mercy and help. This is the core of evensong, a community ritual that is reflective, prayerful and celebrative. In the early church's celebrations of the evening office in parish and cathedral churches, elements of praise, mercy and intercession were common. Usually these included the elements described in Chapter 3:

- a light service (lucernarium)
- the offering of incense in a call for mercy at the end of the day, using Psalm 141
- petitioning the help of the Lord

These elements are sufficient for a prayer service of reasonable length. One must keep these three elements—light service, incense service, intercessions—clearly in mind, understanding and feeling how they interrelate and flow from one another. The notes below are intended to give planners and ministers a sense for the overall structure and the details that make for good liturgy.

All the texts referred to here will be found in *Evening Prayer: The Leader's Book.*

The Light Service (Lucernarium)

We celebrate the redeeming presence of Christ in our midst. We experience that presence in a lighted candle. A darkened space and the presence of the warm glow of the flame are the center of the celebration; the words and music accent and proclaim the ritual action.

The light service begins with the community gathering in a rather dark place. If the group is small, people could gather where the paschal candle is placed, usually at the baptistry. The font could be open with water in it for the people to touch and bless themselves as they arrive. When the paschal candle cannot be used, another candle of worthy stature should be found. If some members of the community usually come early, a few chairs or benches can be ready in the area so that people can rest and collect their thoughts for the service. When everyone has gathered, the presider and any other ministers enter. The presider carries the lighted paschal candle. When the light is in the midst of the assembly, the presider acclaims the presence of Christ, the light:

Jesus Christ is the light of the world!

The community replies:
A light no darkness can overpower!

The candle is placed in its stand; a hymn to Christ, our light, is sung. The ancient hymn, "Phos Hilaron," is the usual choice for this:

O radiant light, O sun divine,
Of God the Father's deathless face,
O image of the light sublime
That fills the heav'nly dwelling place.

O Son of God, the source of light,
Praise is your due by night and day.
Our happy lips must raise the strain
Of your esteemed and splendid name.

Lord Jesus Christ, as daylight fades,
As shine the lights of eventide,
We praise the Father with the Son,
The Spirit blest, and with them one.

16

This hymn is strong in words, rich in imagery, and short enough to be easily memorized. It can be sung to any "long meter" (8, 8, 8, 8) melody; many of these are well known, including some that can be sung in canon or round form (the Tallis' Canon, for example).

To allow time for the community to be caught up in the service, a short pause or a short organ interlude can be placed between the verses of the hymn. Thus one has time to experience in the light the warmth of Christ's presence in the community and the richness of the text.

At the conclusion of the hymn the presider proclaims a solemn prayer of thanksgiving for the light that burns during the night. In form, this prayer is like the blessing prayer over bread and wine at Mass; it is a eucharistic prayer. If the assembly is accustomed to singing the dialogue before the eucharistic prayer at Mass, the presider may use the same melody here to sing: "The Lord be with you," and "Let us give thanks to the Lord our God." The assembly replies as usual, then the presider begins the thanksgiving prayer:

> We praise and thank you, O God,
> for you are without beginning and without end.
> Through Christ, you created the whole world;
> through Christ, you preserve it.
> You are his God and Father,
> the giver of the Spirit,
> the Ruler of all that is seen and unseen.
> You made the day for the works of light
> and the night for the refreshment of our minds and our bodies.
>
> O loving Lord and source of all that is good,
> graciously accept our evening sacrifice of praise.
> You have conducted us through the day
> and brought us to night's beginning.
> Keep us now in Christ,
> grant us a peaceful evening and a night free from sin,
> and bring us at last to eternal life.
> Through Christ and in the Holy Spirit,
> we offer you all glory, honor and worship,
> now and forever. Amen.

Or:

> We praise and thank you, O God,
> through your Son Jesus Christ, our Lord,
> through whom you have enlightened us,
> by revealing the light that never fades.
> Night is falling, and day's allotted span draws to a close.
> The daylight which you created for our pleasure has fully
>   satisfied us;
> and yet, of your free gift,
> now the evening lights do not fail us.
> We praise you and glorify you
> through your Son, Jesus Christ, our Lord,
> through him be glory, power and honor to you
> and the Holy Spirit,
> now and always and forever and ever.
> Amen.

This solemn prayer of thanksgiving concludes the light service. A short pause should follow before beginning the incense service.

Two variations of the light service should be mentioned. In one, the candle may already be lighted as the community gathers for the service, suggesting the abiding presence of the light in our midst. Then the service would begin with the ministers and community gathering about the candle and the presider singing the opening acclamation, "Jesus Christ is the light of the world." Another variation would be to light other candles or to turn up artificial lights during the hymn. This should not distract from the centrality of *the* light as expressed in the paschal candle, but must be seen as the spreading and extension of the light. The action of lighting other candles or lights should also not distract the community in its celebration. These would not be candles held by the assembly but candles placed at various locations around the room. In any case, an atmosphere of dim light throughout the liturgy reminds all that it is evening and that we have one true light.

Incense Service

Asking God's mercy for the sins of the day is the focus of this part of evensong. Placing incense on the burning coals and seeing and smelling the rising smoke ritualizes this. The words of Psalm 141 express the meaning of the ritual action.

Unless the assembly is rather large, the place for the incense service should allow everyone to stand and to come forward to put incense on the coals. Even when the numbers are large, everyone should be able to watch the ascending smoke and smell its sweet odor.

Normally the incense service takes place beside the light, but, in some circumstances, moving to another place will enhance participation in this rite. This can be invited with words as simple as "Let us now ask God for mercy and for protection through the night" and the movement of the presider and ministers is sufficient to effect this. The community would then move in silence to the new place. The next part of the service would begin only after everyone has gathered in the new area.

If the community is not to move to a new place, it is necessary to change the focus of attention by the movement and actions of the ministers and the tone of the music. The short period of silence after the light service helps to indicate a change of focus: one liturgical action has been completed and another is about to begin. Some may feel that this shift of focus within one place is the best way; thus the whole liturgy takes place in the presence of the light.

Coals should be lighted before the service in a brazier which is placed on a table of appropriate size. Instead of a brazier, a bowl that is filled with sand to absorb the heat may be used. The traditional thurible is also a possibility; it is usually open throughout the service and sitting on a table.

No incense is placed on the coals before the service. The table for incense should always be set away from the altar so as not to be associated directly with it. The altar itself is never an appropriate table for the brazier of lighted coals or thurible.

When the assembly is ready for the incense service, the presider places incense on the burning coals in silence. As the smoke begins to rise, the cantor intones the antiphon of Psalm

141: "My prayers rise like incense, my hands like the evening offering." The community repeats the antiphon and the cantor sings the verses:

I have called to you, O Lord;
hasten to help me.
Hear my voice when I cry to you.
Let my prayer rise before you like incense,
and raising of my hands, like an evening oblation.

Set a guard over my mouth, O Lord;
keep watch, O Lord, at the door of my lips!
Do not turn my heart to things that are wrong,
to evil deeds with those who are sinners.

Never allow me to share in their feasting.
If someone good strikes or reproves me it is kindness;
but let the oil of the wicked not anoint my head.
Let my prayer be ever against their malice.

To you, Lord God, my eyes are turned;
in you I take refuge; spare my soul!
Give praise to the Father, the Son, and Holy Spirit.
both now and for ages unending. Amen.

The other ministers and the community may also come forward and place incense on the coals during the psalm. This is not an appropriate time to use the censer to honor the candle, altar or people with incense.

To help pace this rite, the cantor may choose to pause each time between the community's antiphonal response and the next verse. There is no rush. To allow time for all who wish to place incense on the coals, part or all of the psalm may have to be repeated once or twice, or verses from Psalms 140 and 142 may be added as was once the practice in some traditions. However, one must also be aware that length as well as brevity can be awkward and disruptive of the whole service. A good presider makes a careful judgment here. If the presider, ministers and community seat themselves after making an incense offering, an atmosphere of reflection is encouraged. When all are then seated, the cantor or presider can bring this rite to a conclusion. The

20

community, whether seated or standing, should watch the smoke rising and breathe in the sweet odor while reflecting on the words of the antiphon and psalm. The incense service closes with the presider praying in the name of the community and church with words that sum up the ritual action just completed.

The Intercessions

Whenever the Christian community gathers in prayer it makes intercessions for its own needs and the needs of the world. A combination of both formal, prepared intercessions and more personal, spontaneous petitions from the gathered community form the nucleus of this part of the service. Formal sung petitions in the Byzantine tone add solemnity to the rite and establish a certain rhythm as the litany alternates between the leader, usually the cantor, and the community.

A traditional posture of petitioning is kneeling. The rite and posture can be introduced (following a pause after the incense rite) by a sentence such as: "Together with Mary, the Mother of God, and all the saints and with the whole church let us kneel and pray for the needs of the church and the world." Only when everyone has assumed the chosen posture should the petitions begin. During Eastertime, it would be inappropriate to kneel for the intercessions.

When the formal intercessions are finished, the community may be invited to add more personal petitions. Ample time should be given for this. If a prayerful pace has been set, lengthy pauses may occur between the petitions, but people will not feel uneasy about this. On some occasions, the presider may decide that there will be no spontaneous petitions, choosing instead to add the names of the sick and deceased and other particular needs of the world and local community to the formal, sung petitions.

The personal petitions from the community will probably be spoken. If the leader of the formal petitions is confident in singing, he or she may add in song after each of the people's petitions, "Let us pray to the Lord" and the community responds in song, "Lord, have mercy."

The presider will judge when the petitions have finished and conclude with a summary plea for God's assistance. This may be very simple:

> In the communion of the Holy Spirit and of all the saints, let us commend ourselves and one another to the living God through Christ our Lord.

This concluding prayer is ecclesial in nature and the words and tone should reflect this.

Concluding the Liturgy

The liturgy closes with the assembly standing for the Lord's Prayer and a solemn blessing. The blessing, in its words or by its chant, calls for the assembly's "Amen."

After the blessing, the liturgy can conclude with a simple dismissal, "Let us go in peace." The response is "Thanks be to God," and usually an exchange of a sign of peace. This dismissal rite is important if the community is small and there is no formal exit of the ministers.

The community should also be sensitive to the fact that some people may care to pause for a moment of reflection before leaving. The candle and incense should be left in place until everyone leaves and, of course, all should be aware of the need for a quiet atmosphere.

A prayerful celebration of evensong depends greatly on the pacing and modeling done by the ministers and especially the presider. The periods of silence between the various ritual actions, the pace of the movements and the pace of the words whether spoken or sung, the care and grace with which the ritual actions are done: all add or detract from the celebration. The role of the ministers in setting the pace and modeling the proper attitude cannot be overemphasized.

5 ༈

Introducing Evening Prayer

Rite, Ministers and Community

The first step is to have the ministers familiar and comfortable with the material and structure of evensong. This is all the more true when there is only one minister. Such familiarity with the liturgy comes with study, reflection, and use. Singly and collectively the ministers should prepare themselves for the office of evensong: knowing the history, being familiar with the flow of the liturgical actions, texts and music. Experiences of light, incense, body posture and movement are important so that the ministers can set the tone and model the service for the entire community. When the service is a prayer for the ministers of evensong, it will most likely become a prayer for all. The ministers' training could also include praying the liturgy together, even if there are only two or three ministers. While adaptations would have to be made for such a small celebration, the experience of the flow of the service and the ritual actions and symbols would be most valuable.

The rite itself should be marked by simplicity in two ways. First, the flow of the rite should not be obscured. More psalms, prayers or actions or more elaborate "doings" do not necessarily mean a better liturgy. Second, simplicity refers to beginning where the community is. One should use as many of the community's prayer and ritual habits as is possible: the tunes they know, the postures they are accustomed to. Initially teach only what is additionally necessary to celebrate evensong: the opening acclamation, the light hymn, the refrain to the incense psalm, the use of incense and the sung response to the litany. When the community is familiar with the basic structure and flow, one can add other melodies and harmonization, invite the community to use new postures such as bowing for the doxologies and raising their hands at the Lord's prayer. Movement and body posture, harmonization and other additions are always intended to make the basic rite more prayerful. People should never feel that they have to cease praying in order to carry out the ritual. A full evensong service may take years to develop.

Only a short introduction to the meaning of evensong is needed. The ritual should to a great extent explain itself. A few instructions on the movements and a short choir practice—five minutes for all of this—should have a group ready to begin. A few *invitational* instructions ("Let us . . .") during the service should be sufficient to remind the community of what it should do. The first time everything will not be perfect, but the modeling of the actions and attitudes by the ministers and a few reminders and suggestions *before the service* are all that is necessary to have the community celebrating evensong even in the first few experiences. After these initial experiences, practice and instruction will not be necessary. The "veterans" can carry the rite as newcomers learn it.

Occasions for Beginning

Every parish has situations that are ideal for introducing evensong into the liturgical life. One of these is at the opening or closing of various parish committee or society meetings that take place in the afternoon or evening. Whether evensong is celebrated before or after the meeting should be decided by the time of day and the most prayerful time of the meeting. If, as the people come, they are still busy greeting one another and visiting, the meeting would better close with evensong. On the other hand, if people are anxious to leave, it may be more important to begin with it. A pastoral decision is necessary.

Special times of the church year—Advent, Lent and Easter-time—are excellent for beginning evensong in the parish. These seasons call for a special attitude of prayer and usually the Christian community is more inclined to respond. After several years of evensong in these seasons, a parish may consider celebrating evensong every week of the year and perhaps daily during these holy seasons. Once again, make a pastoral judgment.

If evensong has already been introduced to various groups within the parish, the initial steps for publicizing the liturgy for the full parish have already been taken. A brief bulletin announcement and a few words from the pulpit should be all that is necessary. The announcement may read:

> The liturgy of evensong will be celebrated at 5:30 PM each [Sunday, Wednesday, etc.] during the lenten season.
> The evensong liturgy is a prayer praising the redeeming presence of Christ, the light, and asking God's mercy and help. You are invited to celebrate this liturgy.

Neighboring parishes may wish to cooperate with such announcements of evensong during a season like Lent. In some places, Christians of other traditions may be invited also. The best publicity will always be the word-of-mouth recommendation.

What should always be made clear is that evensong is a liturgy of *praise* and *mercy*. One should not try to load it down with additional items or purposes.

Space, Lighting and the Size of the Group

The use of space and lighting is important. A few people in a church that holds a thousand can be devastating to a prayerful service. Gathering people in smaller areas, such as the baptistry or even a small chapel, can create an atmosphere of intimacy, prayer and celebration. A small number offers advantages over the usual crowd at Sunday eucharist. Be aware of the opportunities; think creatively in using space and lighting and in grouping people.

Most of what has been written so far presumes a rather small community celebrating evensong, no more than forty people and more likely ten to twenty. At some point the group may become larger and the active role of the community diminishes: major actions such as the incense rite would then have to be done by the ministers *in the name of the community.* This should be the experience of all who attend.

When the ministers do the ritual actions in the name of the community, it is even more important that they carry out their tasks well. Their movements and gestures must be well planned, practiced and done with grace and decorum. The prayers must be proclaimed in the name of the community while taking note of the difference in proclamation styles: e.g., the thanksgiving prayer is not done in the same way as the final prayer of the incense rite or the intercessions.

Care should be taken that incense is so plentiful that it can be seen and smelled by all. In a very large church there may even be the need to go through the aisles, swinging the censer during Psalm 141. Two or more bowls at different places in a large congregation may be needed so that all can experience the incense by sight and smell. Remember the incense rite is precisely that: the smoke of the incense is to be seen, the odor smelled. Many varieties of incense are available. Sometimes one fragrance will be more fitting for Lent, another for Eastertime.

When a large community gathers for evensong, the challenge is to have the congregation truly involved in the celebration and not there as mere spectators. All should be standing at attention during the light service, experiencing the light of Christ; all should feel that the rising incense is expressive of their prayer for mercy; all should kneel before the Lord begging for the needs of the church and world; all should raise their hands in the prayer our Lord gave us, pleading for the coming of the kingdom. It may be some years before most congregations reach this stage, but the role of the ministers now is to lead the community in celebration. This mission must not make them downhearted because it takes time.

Evensong as a popular form of liturgical prayer will probably be a long time in coming. A small core group may be the most one can expect. Even groups of three or four people need not be discouraging. One should take advantage of such gatherings by allowing the members to take a more active part in

26

the liturgy. They may stand around the candle with the presider, place incense on the coals, join in the intercessions. Be aware of the difference the size of the group makes and use it to the advantage of the prayer.

Ministers

Throughout its history the Christian community has designated certain people to lead the community in prayer. It has done so not to deny access of the individual Christian to the Father, but to acknowledge particular gifts within the community itself. These are gifts given by the Spirit for the upbuilding of the community.

Care has been taken here to speak of the presider, cantor and ministers. Evening prayer does not require the presence of a priest or deacon. Some member of the gathered group, recognized for his or her gifts in leading the community in prayer, may preside. Care should be taken to use the gifts of the individual: the roles of presider and other ministers are not opportunities to give everyone a chance.

The cantor leads the community in psalm, intercession and song. This is a most important ministry at evensong. If no one else is available, the presider can take this role also when the assembly is small.

An assistant to the presider is also helpful. This assistant may carry the candle, give whatever sort of invitational directions are necessary, be of general assistance to the presider.

In a solemn celebration with a large assembly there could be acolytes and a thurifer when such ministers would be helpful during the incense rite. The use of the candle as a symbol of Christ probably makes it inappropriate to have a crossbearer and cross. Similarly, acolytes bearing lighted candles would not accompany this candle.

Recognize the gifts of the community but do not have too many ministers for the size of the group.

Vesture

Vesture is another area where the ministers need to be liturgically sensitive. While the obvious extremes—the parish meeting and the full congregation—provide relatively easy answers, most situations will be in between.

Vesture is part of the service of ministering and celebrating and should not be discarded lightly. It should be in the service of the community's prayer, not a wall between the ministers and the community. Certainly for full solemn celebration with a relatively large group, the presider should wear alb and cope, the deacon his appropriate vesture, the cantor an alb.

Less solemn occasions would probably be reflected in vesture. When evensong is held in a church or chapel, however, the presider would normally be vested in an alb and perhaps the cope; the cantor would probably also wear an alb. One needs a sensitivity to dressing up as a way to add to the celebration.

Additional Psalms and Scripture?

Those who have been praying vespers for some time may feel that they need more psalmody and scripture in evensong. Historically the use of extensive psalmody in the evening office was due to the monastic practice of covering all the psalms within certain time periods. However, we miss the point if we say the psalms should not be used because they are a later addition to evensong.

The first thing is to uphold the principle that evensong has definite elements: light service, incense service and intercessions. Then one can bridge the gap between the need for more scripture and psalms and the basic elements of evensong in one of two ways.

1. A psalm may be added after the incense service is completed. This should be a psalm in character with the service: a psalm of praise such as Psalm 27 ("The Lord is my light and my salvation") or a New Testament canticle, or a penitential psalm such as Psalm 130 ("Out of the depths") or Psalm 91 ("He who dwells in the shelter of the Most High"). One could also add a short, succinct scripture reading after the psalm, just two or three verses that reflect the character of the celebration and/or the season. A period of silent reflection would follow. Always bear in mind that the liturgy of evensong is *not* a liturgy of psalmody and readings.

2. Another solution is to have a period *before* evensong for scripture reading and psalmody. The scripture reading might be

from the lectionary for the day or another reading appropriate to the season. After the reading there could be a period of silent reflection and one or more psalms. The psalms could be sung using a cantor to lead the assembly singing the refrain. Even having a psalm carefully read by one person is possible.

At the completion of this the ministers would leave to vest and make the final preparation for evensong, thus allowing a brief time between the two services and making a distinction between them. On a time schedule, the reading and psalm(s) might begin at 5:10 and end about 5:25 with the liturgy of evensong scheduled to begin at 5:30. This seems to preseve best the need some feel for more scripture and psalmody and yet protect the integrity of evensong. The preliminary prayer time could be announced, but only as preliminary so that everyone understands that evensong, in this example, begins at 5:30 and the earlier prayers have a private, preparatory nature.

A simpler version of the second method involves a short, reflective scripture reading of perhaps five to ten verses from the scripture of the day or from a passage that complements the scripture of the day. This is read before the liturgy of evensong. After the reading the ministers leave and make the final preparations for evensong. Whatever is done should be done with the intention of preserving the integrity of evensong.

When Singing Is Not Possible

The liturgy of evensong is a sung liturgy. The purpose of the singing is "to assist the assembled believer to express and share the gift of faith . . . It should heighten the texts so that they speak more fully and more effectively. The quality of joy and enthusiasm which music adds to community worship cannot be gained in any other way." (*Music in Catholic Worship*, #23)

If, on occasion, the group gathered cannot sing, has no leader of song, does not know the music, or finds the music too difficult, then the texts can be read in a prayerful and reflective way. The acclamation and prayer of thanksgiving should be proclaimed if they are not sung. The hymn and incense psalm can also be read, observing the punctuation and using natural but varied patterns and tones of the voice. Silence in appropriate places and pacing of the read text now becomes all important. Proclaiming and reading in this fashion need not be artificial and filled with the "sing-song" voice associated with certain styles of church oratory. The reader should convey that what is being read is important and relevant for the reader and the community. Anything artificial has no place here! One could also consider doing the incense rite in silence after the presider recites the words of the antiphon while placing the incense grains on the coals.

Again a pastoral decision has to be made. Singing or reading: which will be more effective, edifying and expressive of the celebration? Is the community capable of singing in such a way that it enhances the service for everyone or is the attempt to sing really more of a distraction to a prayerful, celebrative atmosphere?

The People's Prayer

Evensong should have a format that can be easily and quickly memorized by the community, even by those attending only a few times. People should be encouraged to memorize things like the words of the opening hymn and the psalm refrain (let them borrow the evensong cards for a week). The sooner everyone can be freed from having their eyes glued to the page and their hands occupied with papers or cards, the sooner the experience of prayer can come about: mind, body, spirit; intellectual, physical, emotional.

Liturgical prayer should be a freeing experience, even from eyes and hands bound to texts and books. Repetition and simplicity provide this. They allow evensong to be that hinge at the end of the day when the day's activities can be drawn together and presented to God. They allow for the hassle and activity of the day to be consciously put aside while one is caught up in something greater, more important and self-expressive. Repetition and simplicity are bearable when what is repeated is simple but also rich enough and genuine enough to be expressive of one's life from day to day. Basic, genuine symbols and ritual actions, and words richly poetic do this and can bear the burden of repetition.

6 ❧

The Celebration of Morning Prayer

Morning prayer is a time of praise: unconditioned, ego-forgetting praise which glories in creation and the presence of the creating God. We acknowledge the new existence that all things have in Christ, in whom we live, move and have our being.

The quality of morning itself is meditative. Thus the scale of the celebration is kept simple and subtle. There is a time for gathering, a call to prayer, the invitatory psalm (Psalm 95) and thanksgiving prayer, one of the *laudate* (praise) psalms, the intercessions and conclusion.

A candle and a container for holy water are all the setting needs. The candle can be lighted by one of the early risers to provide a visual link to the evening prayer of the previous day. The participants bless themselves with the water when they come in; from the same container the presider will bless everyone at the dismissal. In this action we are reminded of the primeval waters from which the first creation emerged and of the waters of baptism through which we have been re-created.

All of the texts referred to here will be found in *Morning Prayer: the Leader's Book.*

The Gathering
Morning prayer begins in a quiet coming together. This unstructured time encourages a gradual refocusing of attention

and parallels the waking of the day from dark, through dawn and into full light. It parallels also our own waking from sleep. It is a moment for pulling things together before turning to the new day's activity. The sacredness of this waking event is lingered over, to be tasted with a heightened mindfulness. We are a far distance from the Hopi Indians who experience three moments of dawn: purple dawn, when the human silhouette is first clearly outlined; yellow dawn, when the breath can be seen in the cool air; red sunrise, when the person is fully revealed in detail. Such attentiveness basks in a certain kind of leisure.

During this gathering time, one has a breathing space to reflect on the psalms and meditatively pray the scriptures, sharpening one's awareness of the creation taking place in nature and within our own person. It is a fluid time when people are coming in and settling down. In this quiet atmosphere, the sounds of arrival are accepted as normal rather than as intrusive and distracting. The sounds of footsteps and rustling can assure us that we pray-ers are created beings who are most authentically ourselves when gathered as members of a body visible and audible. The sounds remind us that the prayer is *ours* and not an *I/me/mine* affair. (See page 38 for further suggestions on the gathering.)

The Invitation to Common Prayer

At the scheduled time (or when everyone is ready, if such a loose order is possible), the presider stands to call the assembly to pray: "Open my lips, O Lord, and my mouth shall declare your praise." These words are from Psalm 51, David's prayer of repentance. Lips freed to speak praise are the sign of a life which seeks God at its center. Our first words in the morning are an invitation to praise. While saying them, we sign our lips with a cross in a gesture that seems to bless all the words that will come from those lips.

Psalm 95 is the classic invitatory psalm. Several settings are possible according to the varying make-up of the group:

- The scripture text with a responsory. This is the preferred form, but needs a song leader to be done effectively. After the call to prayer, the song leader sings the responsory which is repeated by the assembly. The song leader sings the appropriate verses, with the response sung by all after each verse. Note that some verses are best used only during Lent. Their content makes them particularly suitable for a penitential season.

- A metrical setting. When a song leader is not available or for variety, the assembly can sing this text to a familiar melody. Again, there are verses for Lent only. Although metrical settings of the scripture are more easily sung, they have the weakness of all paraphrases: the original language and imagery are refashioned for the sake of the hymn's meter. The effective use of metrical settings requires a familiarity with the psalm's text which the setting serves to recall.

- A poetic paraphrase. There may be times when no singing is possible. In this case, a reading of a paraphrase with care and in a free-verse style is an alternative.

Recitation aloud by the group is never desirable, whether of the scripture text, the metrical setting or the paraphrase.

The presider then proclaims a solemn prayer of thanksgiving, summing up the whole intent of the morning prayer. Different texts are suggested: daily, Sunday, Eastertime. This prayer is ideally sung or chanted.

When the day is a liturgical feast or has special significance for the local community, an announcement is made before the call to prayer. Although these events may add a dimension or refine the focus of the celebration of *morning* as a creation time, care is needed to avoid letting the festal theme dominate. There is only one exception—Easter, to which every morning owes its character as a memorial. Any morning prayer during the great Fifty Days takes on the special character of this season. It may be that when our sense of morning is securely replanted and again flourishes in our unconscious, a deliberate framing of festal texts can be successfully done. But not yet: much has still to be learned and unlearned.

The Praise Psalms

The community has been standing during this opening section of prayer. When the solemn prayer of thanksgiving is finished, all sit. After a brief pause, one of the *laudate* psalms is sung.

The single response creatures can make to their creator is thankful praise. In this, the human family has a unique task. Created in the divine image, created male and female after the likeness of God, we are the fitting voice among all the other works of God for giving thanks. The psalms named *laudate* or *hallel* (meaning "God be praised!") are some of the most ancient elements in morning prayer. They close the book of psalms in the Bible. In their words we praise God for the creating that was, is and will be. As humans, we know our weakness and limitations, but this does not undermine the truth that we are creation's voice. Our value and dignity were not destroyed by the fall. God's love has opened our lips to proclaim praise.

There are a number of ways to sing the psalms; the desire for simplicity and clarity sets some restrictions, as do considerations about the probable shape of the group at prayer, its music resources and leadership. Each day of the week may be assigned a different psalm, but it isn't feasible to expect the participants to learn a separate setting for each one (nor is this necessary). Instead, consider a psalm text marked for singing by a cantor with a single refrain that can be used by the assembly for whatever psalm is sung. This refrain can be arranged for the cantor and the assembly and is then repeated after each verse.

This verse/refrain pattern should be considered the normal style for using the psalms, even if other psalm tones or settings are introduced. With this form, the cantor can use discretion in the pace of the psalm. For instance, a brief pause after the refrain before the next verse is an effective and reflective pattern, one which moderates our tendency to hurry once we are familiar with a text. It is not inappropriate to have the verses of the psalms spoken, but ending with a cue for singing.

After the closing doxology and refrain, the presider says: "Let us pray." There is a significant silence before the psalm prayer is spoken. This is without any special ceremony. Presider and all remain seated.

Intercessions

As in the evening, the assembled church commends its needs to the compassionate creator. We remember the church itself, the governments and peoples of the world, those present at prayer in this time and place, the sick and the oppressed, the dead—in effect, all those to whom the church is servant.

The shape of these intercessions is variable. The form in which Christ is addressed by different titles (e.g., "Morning Star," "Dawn from on high," "Sun of Justice") enhances the praise character of the petitions and the christological focus of the church's prayer. It is appropriate to our dignity and calling to stand while they are sung. The particular needs of individuals can be spoken without any common response when the general petitions are completed. A commemoration of a saint's feast of the day is also appropriate, as is the recalling of death anniversaries of persons known to the participants.

Conclusion

Morning prayer concludes with the Lord's Prayer, a blessing by the presider of the assembly with holy water and the dismissal. After the blessing, the presider says, "Let us go in peace," and all answer, "Thanks be to God." Or, the presider might say, "Let us offer one another the peace of Christ" and, during the informal exit, people share the kiss of peace.

Once the prayer is finished, any prolonged conversation among the participants should be avoided, respecting the desire of individuals to remain for a time of prayer. The candle and other items are left in place until all are gone. Perhaps the last person can perform this housekeeping service.

7 ಶಿಖ

Introducing Morning Prayer

In addition to the general considerations mentioned in the discussion on evening prayer (see page 23), a number of comments pertinent to morning prayer itself are suggested here.

1. Check out the weekday/weekend patterns of the parish.

Morning prayer is easier for daily scheduling simply because of the extracurricular demands our work and leisure make on the evening hours. Our mornings already have a certain routine built into them and thus may be more adaptable to scheduling common prayer.

2. The number of participants will be relatively small.

One can expect that the elderly will be a majority along with people on the way to work. This requires a realistic view in choosing materials and personnel since number and individuals present affect how well singing is done—morning voices are not very strong or confident.

An ordinary parish of today rarely has, or can expect to have in the near future, the resources presumed in the morning services found in some newer hymnals. Neither the trained leaders nor the community's musical talents are generally available. Thus, the goals at the start should be down-to-earth and modest, directed toward developing content and sensitivity rather than performance.

Reciting the invitatory and alleluia psalms is not too desirable, but full community singing is not always possible for a variety of reasons. An alternative is to learn a few relatively fixed responses: when a cantor is not available, most anyone can stand to speak the verses of the psalm, with the refrain being sung by all. This minimal singing will help preserve the norm of the celebration as *sung*. In any event, a dependable cantor is necessary until the basic patterns and refrains are comfortably in the minds of the participants.

3. Something done daily works differently from something done only occasionally.

Daily ritual action will become familiar and effective when it is kept simple and direct and thoroughly the assembly's. Weak or thematic texts will wear out fast, but those of substance will have time to reveal their depths. Routine can lead to monotony or it can allow a freedom that lets the participants be moved and shaped by the rhythm of prayer. Be ready (but not too soon) to make adjustments for the common good. Be slow to change that which bothers only a few individuals.

4. Provide for the gathering time.

One of the most justified expenditures a parish might make is for a number of psalters and books of selected scripture readings (if possible with large type) for use during the quiet preparatory time. Not all psalms were written for public use. The psalter is too often unknown to most Christians; its use in private prayer and reflection is to be encouraged. The morning serves this purpose well.

5. Morning prayer or Mass?

This question will surely be raised: If people are going to come to church in the morning, why not just celebrate the eucharist? The full response would need a book, but these are the main points to consider:

- Morning prayer has its own quite different focus and content. (Refer to the above discussion on daily prayer as a celebration of time.)

- There is a need to introduce non-eucharistic prayer whose form and content is substantially *liturgical*, i.e., derived from an ecclesial spirituality and involving ritual celebration. We need to recover a sensitivity to *common* prayer and to the particular skills of community celebration. We need keener attention to the symbols which express our prayer. Non-eucharistic ritual prayer can be of great service in this task.

- To an increasing extent, the priest shortage is affecting the availability of daily Mass. A communion service is the usual remedy in many places, but even this is not always possible. Perhaps the celebration of morning prayer is a more suitable alternative.

6. What about additional psalms, scripture readings and the use of traditional New Testament canticles?

A partial response to this question was given on page 28. It is important that an unwarranted load of texts—even traditional ones—not be laid on the participants of morning prayer. But because it is less ceremonial and more reflective, the temptation will be strong. Sustaining the creation/praise motif is essential, as is maintaining a reasonable duration for the sake of people who live with limited, scheduled time. Reflective prayer is not always well served by an abundance of words. This being said, what about a daily scripture reading, the canticle of Zachary (Benedictus) and additional psalms? The reading and psalms could be readily assimilated into the gathering time, presuming they are well chosen for the time of day and appropriate to the season. The canticle of Zachary might be added as a second praise psalm, one that would be used each day. In some respects it works better than the canticle of Mary does in the evening, because of its references to Christ, the "dawn from on high." Perhaps it should only be added when people are completely at home with the rest of morning prayer.

In summary, the place to begin the parish celebration of morning prayer is discovered through a careful look at where one hopes to end: in a prayerful experience which takes seriously this character of morning time and how it works as the natural symbol of the creation event. To do this effectively requires careful attention to the people who choose to gather, to the discipline which simplicity and clarity impose on the selection of materials, and to an awareness of modifications which the experience of the prayer might suggest. A generous amount of patient good humor will soften the firmness needed to preserve the integrity which morning prayer possesses in its own right, but which will always be somewhat elusive. The mystery at the heart of the experience of time is unfolding, ready to be known by those who stop long enough to wonder at it all.

—— Appendix ——

Notes on Evening Prayer
for the Presider

The preceding chapters offer ample information for all involved
in planning and ministering at parish evening prayer. Normally,
the presider would be among the planners as they study and
discuss the structure and celebration presented here for evening
prayer. The following brief notes, then, are not intended to add
anything new. Rather, they summarize for the presider some of
the important points already discussed. They are intended
primarily for situations where the presider has not been able to
take part in the planning and does not have experience with this
order of celebration.

A Sense of the Structure

Have in mind the flow of this liturgy. It is evening. The
community gathers, probably a very small group; some of them
may come early for the reading of scripture or praying of psalms.
When it is time to begin, you bring into the midst of the
community the lighted paschal candle. You acclaim Christ as
light of the world and join in a hymn to Christ our light, then
lead a prayer of thanksgiving which is usually sung.

Mixed with our end-of-day thanksgiving is some frustration,
sorrow, anger. Putting grains of incense on burning coals, you
begin a ritual where the sweet smell and the rising smoke help us
bring all the day's troubles and defeats before the Lord and his
merciful love. With the community you pray Psalm 141 without
hurry as the smoke of the incense rises.

Finally, you or the cantor initiate and conclude the prayer of intercession. Be aware that, however few we may be, we are the church that is to intercede with the Lord, praying for all the needs of the world. Our evening prayer ends quietly with the Lord's prayer and a blessing.

The praise and thanks around the light, the offering of incense in quiet reflection, the unhurried prayers of intercession: these are the moments of evening prayer.

Pace

Nothing need be hurried. In the light service, the hymn will begin immediately after the acclamation. After the hymn, let there be a brief pause before beginning the thanksgiving prayer. A longer pause should separate this prayer from the incense service, but in that pause you will approach the brazier, and ask all present to pray together for God's mercy. Then, in silence, you place incense on the coals and watch in silence as the smoke begins to ascend. Only then will you or the cantor begin Psalm 141.

The singing of Psalm 141 may allow for times of silence between the verses; after the psalm, if there is to be a concluding prayer, you will invite all to pray and then pause for a fairly long time before speaking the prayer.

The intercessory prayers may have a different pace. If they are sung, as suggested, this litany-like prayer should move along rapidly, with cantor and assembly overlapping each other. If there are also to be prayers from the assembly, the pace should be slow and relaxed so that people will feel completely free to pray aloud and in their hearts. Make a short pause after the concluding prayer of the intercessions, then begin the Lord's prayer and go on to the blessing. Even the peace greeting, if used to conclude, is quiet and serves as an unhurried transition from the prayer.

Movement and Gesture

Be aware of every movement. They are not many. At the beginning, you carry the lighted paschal candle into the assembly. This is done with great reverence for light and for the people. You hold the candle high as you acclaim: "Jesus Christ is

42

the light of the world!" And keep it held high as the assembly responds and as the hymn begins. During the hymn you place the candle in the candlestand and stand near, facing it, singing. During the thanksgiving prayer, the book would normally be held by an acolyte or by one of the assembly so that you can stand with hands open as during the eucharistic prayer at Mass.

The placing of the incense on the coals is also done with reverence: an awareness of the beauty and power of fire, of the delight of the sweet smell of the incense, of the great unhurriedness of this day-ending time when we can actually take time to do nothing more useful than watch smoke rise and let its good odor fill us. Your attitude throughout the incense service should be such that no one feels rushed.

During the intercessions you simply take part as one of the assembly. The only gestures here would be kneeling, if this is done, and in rising at the conclusion. The blessing at the end of the service could be given with arms fully extended.

In the silent parts, remember to be still: do not turn pages or look around to the cantor or acolyte. Just keep a prayerful silence.

As presider, you minister to the assembly *as a member of the assembly*. Especially when the gathering is small and when the cantor shares the leadership, you simply pray as any other person during much of the liturgy.

When you invite people to acclaim the light, to give thanks, to pray, to join in intercession, you do this by gesture and example as well as by word. All of these must go together. When you speak such invitations, be sure that they not only sound like invitations, but look like invitations: by your posture of arms and hands, the eyes.

Eventually, some groups may wish to use other gestures in evening prayer. For example, you and all in the assembly might stand with hands folded in the traditional way during Psalm 141. Each time the refrain is sung, open your hands and slowly raise them. Hold the arms high until the refrain is finished, then slowly return to the "folded hands" posture as the cantor sings the next verse.

Presiding

No amount of knowledge of a liturgical rite can substitute for the true charism of the presider. The presider is not here "in the midst of the assembly" to do what is in the book or what he or she has memorized. The presider has memorized the rite so that there is freedom to discern the movement of prayer in this assembly. The presider is to serve the prayer by being thoroughly at home within it. Presiding is a true service to the community's prayer, not merely an official role to be filled. In initiating a regular parish practice of evening prayer, all—presider and everyone else—will be learning to be assembly, learning to be presider. It will take some time. This may be facilitated if small groups pray evening prayer at home or in the rectory, perhaps at the dinner table, using at least some elements of the service as outlined here. Out of this learning, out of time spent in silent praise of God for all that evening means and does, comes the prayer of a community.